Spectacular Service

Spectacular Service

Transforming Transactions into Relationships

Scotty Werner

Copyright © 2019 Scotty Werner
All rights reserved.

ISBN-13: 9781706247548

FOREWORD

You are about to embark on a journey that will transform the way you and your company approach customer service. At the helm of the ship for this journey is Scotty Werner. Scotty has been a friend and mentor to me for more than 20 years. Over that time, I have watched him grow as a friend, a leader, a public speaker, an author, and as one of the nation's foremost experts in helping companies deliver amazing customer service experiences.

As you enjoy your way through this book, I encourage you to think about your own experiences with customer service. Have you ever stopped doing business with a company that let you down? Have you ever become loyal to a company because of a positive experience? Scotty's easily relatable anecdotes demonstrate how poor customer service can impact consumers and affect the bottom line of both large and small companies. According to American Express, more than half of Americans have stopped doing business with a company due to bad customer service. Applying the lessons in this book will help you avoid becoming a victim of that statistic.

Scotty and I began our careers in customer service together in the late 1990s at the investment brokerage firm Charles Schwab, Inc. The tech bubble had the market in a manic froth, and clients were clamoring for information about their accounts. To handle the volume of calls, Schwab was hiring dozens of new customer service representatives every week. With his positive attitude and passion for delivering quality service, Scotty stood out from both new hires and seasoned professionals. He led by example, motivating fellow employees during the most difficult periods. I clearly remember a day in late 2000 when the tech bubble was in the midst of bursting. With hundreds of phone calls from anxious clients waiting on hold, Scotty was a beacon of calm, encouraging his colleagues to treat each phone call as an opportunity to help a worried, emotional client through a tough time.

During those early years at Schwab, Scotty was building the foundation for a career in customer service that has spanned multiple industries, from financial services to hospitality. He has developed techniques and best practices that can be applied to any type of business. Scotty's focus on the customer experience regardless of industry earns him the authority to write this book.

Scotty is the kind of person who can accomplish anything he sets his mind to. He is the author of the bestselling book Caddy Tales, a three-time World Bench Press Champion, and an Iron Man finisher. Scotty completed an Iron Man triathlon (the full one that consists of a 2.4-mile swim, a 112-mile bike ride, and a 26-mile run) in Panama City, Florida, in November of 2017. Eight months later, he underwent a six-arterial bypass surgery. Think about what it takes to complete an Iron Man race, then compound that with a bad heart. His own doctors could not believe it, but it is the truth. The positive attitude and determination that drove Scotty to achieve those impressive milestones are the same forces that he applies to his passion for coaching and teaching spectacular customer service.

Because Scotty has personally taken over 250,000 customer service calls and trained more than 3,000 customer service professionals, he can speak from personal experience. His stories illustrate the opportunities that companies have to influence customer experience during routine transactions. Unfortunately, there is a lot of room for improvement!

The news on the customer service front is not all bad, however. In many chapters, Scotty highlights outstanding service, showing how it can drive client loyalty, increase customer base, and impact the bottom line. My personal favorite is Chapter 7, which focuses on employee empowerment. Here Scotty unfolds a story about a series of customer service encounters within one business. The overall message is that a corporate culture of providing exceptional service is a key factor in becoming a world class company.

Along with the stories, Scotty includes actionable practices that you can put in place today to improve customer service in your company. Check out SAINTS in the opening chapter, the simple yet time-tested techniques that can have dramatic results not just in business, but in your everyday life. You will also find great tips in the Appendix, one of which may have you searching for notepaper and a stamp every Friday.

I do not know anyone more talented or more focused on transforming transactions into relationships than Scotty Werner. I am convinced that if you follow the practices that Scotty lays out in this book, you will be well on your way to developing relationships with customers who would not even consider doing business with your competitors. You will put customer transactions in your past, and your future will be fully comprised of client relationships.

Enjoy,

Scott Connor, CFA, CFP, MBA

DEDICATION

This book is dedicated to my friends and family. You have always been there and continue to support me in my every endeavor, no matter how crazy. Over the years, I have leaned on you more than humanly possible and, in every instance, you stood by my side with encouragement, support and guidance. A sincere thank you does not even scratch the surface when it comes to sharing my gratitude with all of you.

Table of Contents

PREFACE .... **XIII**

INTRODUCTION TO SAINTS **1**

MOE'S SOUTHWEST GRILL **3**

MEN'S WAREHOUSE **5**

QUAN, THE DUCT MAN **6**

THE MARRIOTT MILE **10**

ZAPPOS (BEEP-BEEP-BEEP) **13**

THE RITZ (EMPLOYEE EMPOWERMENT) **17**

INSURANCE (SWING AND A MISS) **24**

CARMAX (THAT WAS EASY) **27**

APPLE (ARE THEY PSYCHIC?) **30**

DOCTORS AND NURSES **32**

FREEDOM BOAT CLUB (I GOT YA!) **38**

HOME DEPOT (LET ME GET THAT) **41**

SOUTHWEST AIRLINES (KICK TAIL®) 43

MARRIOTT (SKILLET MEATBALLS) 45

SPLASHEO (IT'S DONE?) 47

TIME SAVER (CALL ME) 50

PUBLIX (SHE FOUND ME) 52

FRESHLY (NO HUMANS?) 54

CARNIVAL CRUISE LINE 56

AMEX (WE WILL FIND A SOLUTION) 58

TOP CUSTOMER SERVICE TIPS 60

CUSTOMER SERVICE FACTS 64

PREFACE

I enjoy seeing people succeed. If I can help in that process, it puts a smile on my face. Some have told me that I am a good storyteller and I should share those stories with others. To me, that sounded like a good idea only if I could help others through my storytelling. That is when Spectacular Service was born.

I genuinely believe that people all over the world want to deliver great service. The challenge in this hectic world is that, sometimes, managers and leaders don't have the time it takes to coach, teach, and mentor their teams. Individuals and companies are thirsting for knowledge to help them differentiate themselves from the competition, but are challenged to find specific, actionable best practices they can put in place to stand out instead of blending in. Spectacular Service: Transforming Transactions into Relationships is a collection of stories that detail how companies and individuals make this leap.

Scotty Werner

scottywerner.com

INTRODUCTION TO SAINTS

Throughout this book, you will see how the acronym SAINTS is used to build a foundation in each story that leads to a spectacular customer experience. How did SAINTS come about? Well, whenever I delivered a presentation or a workshop, I discussed "the six surprisingly simple, yet time-tested techniques used to deliver spectacular service," however, I never had an acronym for them. Those six techniques were uncovered by telling powerful and entertaining stories.

While I was speaking in Tampa, Florida, one of the audience members came up to me and said the presentation was excellent. I asked what I might do to improve it for the next group. He mentioned that he enjoyed everything, however, he really wished I had an acronym to help him remember the six techniques. The next day, SAINTS was born.

SAINTS stands for:

Smile - the most powerful gesture in the world.
Actively Listen - by actively listening to people, you engage them in deeper, more meaningful conversations.
Important - make the other person feel important.
Name - remember and use a person's name as often as possible.
Talk - talk about items that are important to your conversation partner. Talking about topics that interest others helps you transform a transaction into a relationship.
Sincere - be sincere, authentic and genuine.

As you read through this book, notice how individuals use SAINTS in their own personal way to deliver spectacular service. I hope that you enjoy the stories and come away with some specific techniques that you can put in place to help transform a transaction into a relationship. Who knows? Maybe the next edition of Spectacular Service will be about one of your customer service experiences.

MOE'S SOUTHWEST GRILL

I was in Atlanta during January when the weather became extreme very quickly. On my way home from work, I heard advisory warnings on the radio. Now I live in Florida, so weather warnings are nothing new to me, but we have hurricanes, not snow and ice storms. As the advisories became more serious, a city-wide curfew was finally announced. That's right, the city I was in had a curfew until 4 p.m. the following day. Wow!

Pretty soon, Atlanta looked like a ghost town. Businesses closed early so employees could get home before the curfew began. The staff at the Marriott where I was staying remained on the job, planning to stay in the hotel's vacant rooms. I passed the time that evening working out on the treadmill, hitting the weights, and watching movies in my room.

When the curfew ended the next afternoon, I went to the front desk and asked for a recommendation for dinner. Without hesitation, two of the employees responded simultaneously, "Moe's!" They said it with such passion that I thought they could be investors in the company.

Because the restaurant was only a short distance away, I braved the cold weather and walked. As soon as I entered the building, everyone called out, "Welcome to Moe's!" And I mean everyone, including the customers. I immediately felt as if I were an important person, like a family member. What a tremendous feeling. After placing my order, I took a seat and enjoyed the atmosphere. The food was fantastic, the service was spectacular, and the employees were authentic and genuine. Starting with the greeting I received when I walked in, Moe's created an experience that ensured a customer for life.

When I got home, I told this story to a few friends. They mentioned that there are other companies that do the same thing, including the place where I get my hair cut. "How can that be?" I thought. I am a regular and I never even noticed.

Well, sure enough, I paid attention on my next visit. As I walked in the door, some employees (not all) managed a robotic and mandatory, "Welcome." It was not the authentic and genuine greeting I received at Moe's.

I thought about why the same procedure had such a different impact on me. I believe that the manager of the franchise hair-cut place simply instructs employees to say hello to clients as they come in the door. Contrast that with the leadership at Moe's, who seem to recruit front-line personnel that fit the company's energetic and outgoing identity.

Thank you, Moe's, for being authentic and genuine while providing spectacular service.

MEN'S WAREHOUSE

My friend Cameron, who is a great dresser with fantastic taste, needed some new clothes. Shopping online at Men's Warehouse, he noticed a "buy one and get two pair for free" special on pants. Sounds like a great deal. I wish he had let me know about it.

While placing his order, Cameron paid an additional $12 to have the pants hemmed. When the clothes arrived, the quality was excellent and the material was fantastic, however, the slacks were not hemmed. A call to customer service connected Cameron with an agent named Tamika. Apologizing for the mistake, Tamika showed empathy and offered a variety of options to resolve the issue.

Cameron chose the option of going to the local Men's Warehouse store to have the pants hemmed. "There will be no charge for the alterations," Tamika said, "and we'll issue a credit for the original $12 to make up for your inconvenience." As if that were not enough, she said she was sending Cameron a $50 Men's Warehouse gift card.

Tamika's solution showed that she realized, as does Men's Warehouse, that it costs 700% more to acquire a new customer than it does to keep an existing one. By going above and beyond, she helped ensure that Cameron would continue to be a good customer and possibly share his spectacular experience with others.

QUAN, THE DUCT MAN

I woke up in a horrible sweat. It was 1:30 a.m. on a Saturday morning in August, the dead of summer in Florida. There could only be two reasons for my soaked sheets. Either I had the flu, or my air conditioner was broken. Praying to a higher power that I had the flu, I checked the thermostat and saw the number 88. I knew I was in trouble. "Do I have enough money in my 401K to pay for a technician on the weekend?" I thought. Heck, could I even find a technician on a hot summer Saturday?

My fears faded a bit when I heard the fan running. I am not much of a "fix it" guy but I could check a few obvious things. Was the filter clogged? Was the circuit breaker tripped? They were both fine and that was the extent of my mechanical ability. I went back to bed until early morning, trying to decide what to do. Then I thought of Leo, my next-door neighbor who really can fix things. He came over right away and checked the circuit breaker, fan, drainage and filter. Everything seemed okay. "There's only one thing for you to do to," Leo said. "Call Quan, the Duct Man."

I asked Leo for an explanation. "Not necessary," he said, walking away. "I'll text you the number. Just make the call."

By now it was early afternoon and the house was getting hotter by the minute. My call to Quan went right to voicemail. I had three options: leave a message, call the office, or call an emergency number. I did not think it was an emergency, so I left a message and hoped for a return call in the next 48 hours.

As soon as I hung up, my phone rang. It was Quan. We talked for a few minutes, exchanging pleasantries about our mutual friend Leo. Quan asked how Leo was doing and if he was back from his trip to Greece. I said Leo was doing awesome and he returned about a week ago. For some reason, my air conditioner problem was forgotten momentarily while we talked about Leo's trip to Greece. Then Quan walked me through a few items to check, none of which worked. "Don't worry," he assured me, "I'll have someone over there right away. We'll get your house cooling down in no time." Before we proceed, I will let you in on a little fact. Even before Quan called me back, he had made some changes to his team's schedule, so that Tim, a senior technician, would be on his way in case the basic fixes did not work.

As soon as I hung up the phone with Quan, Tim called me. He was already in route to my home. Not getting ready to go, not just leaving a prior customer, Tim was on the way. Fantastic! But how much would such speedy service cost me?

When Tim arrived, he mentioned that he and Quan had installed the air conditioning system two years ago when the house was being built. He told me a story about Quan not feeling well one day while they were working. "He took a short break in the shade," Tim said, "but he kept going so we would meet the deadline."

After we got to know one another a little, Tim started his diagnosis. Ten minutes later, he said, "Scotty, I have good news and bad news. The good news is you have a bad capacitor, but it's only a few dollars. The bad news is that I don't have one on the truck or in the shop."

Offering to call some local distributors to see if he could find the part, Tim soon had better news. He found one. "Great," I thought to myself, "the part will be in California. After I pay for next-day-air shipping charges, and he installs it, I'm going to be broke." Well, the news turned from good to great when Tim said he found the part at a shop about ten miles away and would go get it right away. The AC unit would be up and running in no time. I looked at the thermostat. 138 degrees. Tim was now my new best friend.

While Tim was gone, Quan called to ask how things were going. Are you kidding me? Here is the CEO calling me on a Saturday, in August, to find out how I am doing. This was incredible service. I asked him about what happened when he originally installed the system and fell ill on the job. Quan shared that they had so many installations, he and his team were working 18-hour days. The heat and long hours finally caught up with him, but after an hour break and a gallon of water, he was revitalized and ready to go. Quan said I was in good hands with Tim, but if I needed anything, to call him personally. I was impressed.

I did not know Tim was back until he knocked on the door. "Scotty, we're all finished. Let's look at your thermostat." The temperature had dropped 10 degrees! It was working! Tim went to write up the invoice as I looked at my watch. The entire episode only took two hours. I was amazed, but then my thoughts turned to the bill. How much was this going to cost? This company seemed to drop everything they were doing to take care of me. Was it because of Leo? Was it because they felt it was an emergency? Was it because they thought they owed me something because they installed the original system? The bill was going to be huge. I decided to brace myself and be thankful that someone came on a hot Saturday in Florida to fix it.

Tim came back in, handing me the bill. Whew! Completely reasonable. I took a deep breath knowing that my 401K was safe. Mentioning that there were different payment options, Tim suggested I call Karen in the office to find out my choices. Really? I was a brand-new client and no payment was required immediately after services were rendered? Extremely trusting. After we said our goodbyes, Tim was off to save another customer from sweltering heat.

I phoned Karen to take care of the bill, choosing the option to pay by credit card. "Uh, Scotty," she said, "I don't think you want to do that. The credit card company charges us 3% which, unfortunately, I must pass on to you."

"Karen," I said, "I really appreciate you looking out for me and saving me money. What do you suggest I do?" She recommended that I use my bank's bill pay service, saving the 3% credit card fee and the cost of postage.

This was nothing short of incredible! They had never done business with me before, yet they were trying to save me money while extending credit terms. Unbelievable. I told Karen I was so thankful to have the air conditioner fixed, I wanted to complete everything right then, so I paid with a credit card in spite of the fee.

You may think the story ends here, but it does not. On Sunday, I got a phone call from guess who? That's right, Quan, the Duct Man. He wanted to follow up to see how everything went and if I had any suggestions about how he could improve service in the future. Spectacular! Based on my experience, Quan and his team are already experts when it comes to customer service. They anticipate needs and go above and beyond to exceed expectations, putting the customer first and creating client loyalty and retention. Thank you, Quan, and your entire team, for delivering spectacular service!

THE MARRIOTT MILE

My friend Scott was training for a 10K race. Now if you are a road warrior like he is, getting a three to five mile run in can be a bit of a challenge. Speaking from personal experience, when I travel, I sometimes order room service and watch a movie instead of exercising. Avoiding a workout can become a game with me. What excuse can I use this time?

On this particular trip, Scott was staying at a Marriott hotel in Sarasota, Florida. The Marriott has a worldwide reputation for excellent service, well known for taking routine guest requests and trying to exceed expectations.

When Scott checked in, Kristen at the front desk asked if there was anything else she could do to make his stay more enjoyable. "I want to go for a four-mile run," Scott said, "somewhere outside instead of on a treadmill." Personally, I like the treadmill because I can watch TV and keep my pace consistent, but Scott enjoys being outdoors and listening to music.

Kristen told him that many guests use a route that is close to the hotel, has a great view and is easy to navigate. She began with the directions. "When you go outside, turn right and go about one-half mile down the sidewalk until it comes to a dead end. Make another right, go another half mile, then turn right again at the blue Chase Bank ATM overhang. Continue for one mile along the beach sidewalk until you come to a giant wall. That will make two miles. Turn around there, and when you arrive back at the hotel, you will have nailed your four-mile run for the day."

Thanking her, Scott caught the elevator to his room. After changing clothes and selecting music for his run, he returned to the lobby. Kristen called to him as he crossed the marble floor, "Have a great run, Scott." Someone else was also encouraging Scott. It was the hotel manager, Jeffery.

Rain storms appear like clockwork during summer afternoons in Florida, so Scott was on the lookout for dark clouds as he headed out the door. He figured that if a storm did pop up, he would be back at the hotel before it started. Unfortunately, he was wrong.

Making great time on the first leg of his run, Scott came to the dead end and took a right turn. He continued to follow Kristen's directions as he took in the beautiful scenery during the beach part of his route. But at the giant wall, the halfway point, Scott turned around and knew he was in trouble. Apparently, Mother Nature did not have the same timeframe in mind for the storm as Scott did. It was coming, and it was coming fast. Even at a blazing nine-minute per mile pace, Scott knew he would never make it back to the hotel without getting soaked.

Maybe he could get as far as the Chase ATM overhang and wait out the storm. With legs pumping like pistons, Scott reached it just seconds before the skies opened. The shelter provided some cover from the rain and a sense of accomplishment, but he still had one mile to go and it looked as if this storm was going to stay for a while.

Decisions, decisions, decisions. Stay under the safety of the overhang, or walk back to the hotel while the rain was coming down in sheets? Before Scott could make up his mind, a van pulled to the curb and stopped. The driver rolled down the window. It was Jeffery, the Marriott manager. "Hi Scott, want a ride back?"

"Absolutely!" Scott said, relieved to be rescued from the storm. Hopping out with an umbrella, Jeffrey escorted him to the van, where dry towels and a bottle of water were waiting. They were back at the hotel in a few minutes, without one raindrop hitting Scott.

This is a great example of going above and beyond for a client and exceeding expectations. By actively listening, the Marriott team put a plan in place that delivered spectacular service to a guest. And, if I know Scott, he went down to the treadmill and finished the last mile of his run.

ZAPPOS (BEEP-BEEP-BEEP)

Looking for something new to read, I picked up Delivering Happiness: A Path to Profits, Passion, and Purpose, by Tony Hsieh, the CEO of Zappos. It is awesome. I recommend that you pick up a copy of Tony's book after you finish this one. He includes ten reasons why you should read it, but I think there are many more. I will not spoil any of the chapters, but I think you will like learning about the worm farm and the llama.

Reading Tony's book inspired me to work harder and look for new ways to exceed client expectations. Sometimes I get my best inspiration while exercising, so I put on my running shoes and hit the road. Unfortunately, the only thing I was inspired to do on this particular day was order a new pair of shoes. Mine were worn out. I am usually better about having decent running gear. Time to fix that problem.

I signed into my Zappos account, found a pair of running shoes with a cool orange stripe, and clicked away. My confirmation said the shoes would be here in two days, but it was wrong, dead wrong. The shoes arrived the very next day! Talk about underpromising and overdelivering. This made me feel as if I were Zappos' most important customer. I put the shoes on right away and went for a five-mile run. The endorphins were kicking in, inspiring me to do another customer service video for my company.

The next day was going to be busy, so I wanted to knock out my run first thing in the morning. As I was lacing up my new shoes, one of the eyelets broke. Darn, this was inconvenient. I could still tie the laces, but now my foot wobbled in the shoe. No worries, there are worse things in life than a broken eyelet on a new pair of shoes.

When I arrived back home, I realized that I should have two pairs of running shoes in case something like this happens again. I logged into my Zappos account and placed another order. At the same time, I was able to print a return label to send back the defective shoes. The process was extremely easy and took less than a minute. After packing up the shoes in the original box and attaching the UPS label, I drove to a shipping store to drop off the package. That is when some Zappos magic happened.

I am probably not the only person who thinks that returning merchandise is a pain. It can be difficult to get a return number, you have to take the box to be shipped, then wait for it to travel across the country, get checked in and processed. You hope your credit shows up a few weeks later.

Zappos made the process so easy. When I dropped off my return, the clerk asked if I wanted a receipt. I said sure. He scanned the box...BEEP, then went over to the computer. Another...BEEP and he handed me the receipt. "Thank you," I said and walked out the door. About 18 seconds later, my phone went...BEEP. It was a message from my credit card company. I received a credit for $64.80 to my account. Not something was pending, it was an actual credit!

This company took all the discomfort and friction out of returns. No waiting for the box to fly across the country. No waiting for the warehouse to process the return. No waiting for my money. This was without a doubt the most fun I have ever had returning a product. Kudos to the entire team at Zappos for eliminating a customer pain point.

After reading Tony Hsieh's book and having this experience, I wanted to learn more about Zappos. I found out that the company offers public tours of its headquarters in Las Vegas. Count me in. I already had a trip planned to Vegas for another event, so I added a tour of Zappos to my agenda.

My tour was scheduled for 3 p.m. The instructions said to arrive 30 minutes early, so I did exactly that and was joined by five other people. We each signed paperwork vowing not to reveal any confidential information and promising to have fun while we were there, then we watched a cool documentary about Zappos. Our tour guide was Ryo, a friendly guy with a knowledge of the Zappos culture that was uncanny. You would have thought this guy was one of the nicest people you have ever met.

As we walked through the various parts of the building, I noticed one thing seemed to be missing no matter where we went—employee stress. Could this company actually operate stress free? Even in the Human Resources department, where challenging issues meet strict policy, the team was positive and upbeat. How do they do it? I think Zappos must have a laser focus on the client and company culture. It was extremely impressive.

A few things are stamped in my memory from the end of the tour. The first is an area I call "sleeping with the fishes." I know this may make you think of a certain mobster movie, but this place could not be more different from that scene. Six lounge chairs recline all the way back, allowing you to look up at the ceiling, which is a large, peaceful fish tank. As you relax in the recliners, fish of all sizes, shapes and colors swim right past your head. Any stress you feel would surely dissolve here. Hats off to Zappos for the attention to employee wellness.

The final stop of the tour was the customer service area. Ryo showed us three statistics: the average time to answer a call, the total number of calls answered in the last 24 hours, and the longest call of all time.

All the statistics were incredible, but the longest call was beyond belief. Before you read further, I challenge you to take a guess. Trust me, you will not even be close, so add at least three hours. The amazing part of this statistic is that Zappos "wants" employees to break this record. In a time when most companies try to shuffle off the customers and move to the next transaction, it was refreshing to see Zappos trying to genuinely build relationships. Zappos is proud to announce their longest call was five hours and 32 minutes. That is correct; it is not a typo. Five hours and 32 minutes. What is even more amazing than the length of the call is the way it evolved. Here is the backstory.

The customer service agent noticed that the client was ordering the same products she purchased only a month ago. While keying in the order, the agent told the customer that she must have been pleased with the previous order since she was purchasing the same items again. Sounding emotional, the caller said, "My house burned down. We lost everything."

At the end of the long conversation that ensued, the agent knew that his caller was facing a daunting future. "Don't worry about paying for this order," he said. "This one's on us." What a great story of empowerment and empathy.

From the spectacular customer service, to Tony Hsieh's book, to the tour of the facility, one word comes to mind when I reflect on these experiences...Wow!

THE RITZ (EMPLOYEE EMPOWERMENT)

Needing to do more research for my Keynote presentations, I wanted to work in a mini-vacation at the same time. I decided to book a weekend at the Ritz Carlton Grande Lakes in Orlando, Florida. The Ritz has always been known for its spectacular service, so it seemed like the ideal place to accomplish both goals.

When the weekend finally arrived, I packed my suitcase, grabbed a soda from the refrigerator, and jumped in my car. I live in a small town just north of Orlando, Mount Dora, so it was only a 45-minute drive. Pulling into the Ritz, I noticed a young man coming to greet me. His name tag said Anaro. "Good afternoon, Anaro," I said. "My name is Scott Werner and I'm here for a little weekend vacation."

"Welcome, Mr. Werner, let me take your bag." he replied. "If you'll follow me, I'll get you checked in." As I guzzled down the last drop of soda, I followed Anaro inside, my head swiveling to look for a trash can, which was not lost on my guide. "I'll take care of that for you," he said, as he handed me off to Brittney at the front desk. "Your bags will be waiting for you in your room."

"Good afternoon, Mr. Werner, how can I help you today?" asked Brittney.

I started out by asking a favor. "Mr. Werner sounds a little too businesslike for a weekend getaway. Could you and your team just call me Scott or Scotty?" Brittney asked me which one I preferred and the difference between the two.

"Well, when people first meet me, they call me Scott. After a day, a week, a month, or a year, once we become friends, then they magically just add a "y" to the end of my name."

"Then I hope we earn the opportunity to call you Scotty before you leave."

"Let's start the friendship right now, Brittney. You and your team can call me Scotty."

Finishing up the check-in details, Brittney handed me the electronic credential for the room and offered a glass of lemonade or champagne. Which one do you think I chose? Well…we will find out the answer to that question a little later in the story.

I took my drink and key card, catching the elevator to the 10th floor. About halfway down the hallway, I saw an employee coming towards me. When I got close enough to see her nametag, I said, "Hey, Claudia."

"Hi, Scotty!" Instinctively, we both raised our hands and gave each other a high five.

I realized that although I had only been there for a short while, the staff was already using some of the surprisingly simple, yet time-tested techniques to deliver spectacular service. First of all, everyone was smiling at me and it felt great. A smile is the most powerful gesture in the world. They were also listening, actively listening, to what was important to me. I already felt as if I were the most important person in the hotel.

That evening, I had dinner reservations in the hotel's Grill Room for three guests and me. Our waiter's name was Frank. He took our orders right away as he could see we had already made our dinner selections. When Frank came back, my companions and I were engaged in deep conversation (we were trying to figure out what to do for the weekend).

"I'm afraid we have a small problem, gentlemen." Frank explained that a party of 10 came in after we did, but somehow their order was put in first. Our meals would be delayed by at least

20 minutes. "May I offer you a complimentary bottle of wine for your inconvenience?" he asked. You betcha!

Later, I did some digging and found out that every employee at the Ritz Carlton, from someone who just started to the CEO, is empowered to spend up to $2,000 per day on a guest to fix an unlikely mistake or enhance the customer's experience. The Ritz empowers its employees to take care of guests because they know it costs over 700% more to acquire a new client than it does to keep an existing one. Frank was an ambassador of this statistic.

The next morning, I hopped out of bed early and put on my running gear. I was training for an Ironman and did not want to miss a workout day. After a little stretching (very little), I headed downstairs where I saw a familiar face working the front desk. "Don't you ever go home, Brittney?" I joked. Smiling, she asked what was on my agenda for the day.

"I'm training for an Ironman, so first up is a six-mile run. Next, the lazy river is calling my name. At 1:00, I'm meeting my friend Jason for a tennis match and I'm going to beat the pants off him. After that...who knows?"

"Have a great run, Scotty, and congratulations on your book going to number one," Brittney said. I froze in my tracks. The hairs on the back of my neck stood up. As I turned around, my shoulders rolled back, and my chest filled with pride. "How did you know about that? I don't even tell people I wrote a book."

"Scotty, we take pride in learning a little bit about our guests. Congratulations! Have a great run."

Needless to say, that exchange made me feel fantastic. By using my name, talking about things that were important to me, and being sincere, Brittney was helping to transform a transaction into a relationship. I felt as if I were on top of the world. Instead of running six miles that morning, I went ten.

After the run, I crossed through the lobby and headed toward the elevator. I hopped in, pushed the button, and it whisked me away to the 10th floor. When the shiny doors opened, I made a quick right and an immediate left. Who do you think I saw in the hallway again? That's right, Claudia. We gave each other another high five. This reminded me of a movie called The Truman Show, where every character was perfectly placed to make sure that Jim Carey felt very important. I thought the Ritz was doing the same thing for me.

I grabbed my gear for the lazy river, slipped on my flip flops, and headed down to the pool. A nice young man named Rene came up and introduced himself. "Good afternoon, Scotty. How was your run for your Ironman? Can I bring you something to drink, perhaps a Pepsi® or a lemonade?"

"The run was great, thank you, Rene. I was supposed to go six miles, but I was feeling great, so I went 10. I would love an ice-cold Pepsi®."

"My pleasure," Rene said, galloping away to get my beverage.

"What kind of space-age communication technology does this company have?" I wondered. Everyone knows my name, everyone knows what I am doing, and how in the world did he know to offer me a lemonade or Pepsi®? Then I realized that when Anaro asked me for the soda can to throw away, he must have made a note in their client relationship management (CRM) tool that it was a Pepsi®. Brittney must have done the same thing. When she offered me champagne or lemonade, she made a note in the CRM that I chose lemonade.

After Rene brought my drink, I kicked off my flip flops and started floating. When my fingertips and toes turned into what looked like dried prunes, I figured it was time to get out. As I climbed up the ladder, I noticed that someone had turned around my flip flops so I could slide right into my shoes when I stepped out of the lazy river. Very cool. I saw another ice-cold beverage waiting for me at my lounge chair. This team really knew how to anticipate a guest's needs.

By this time, it was nearly 1:00, time to meet Jason for tennis. I had mentioned to him earlier in the week that I would meet him at the Ritz Kids. I asked Rene how to get there. "Follow me, Scotty, I will show you the way." Rene was kind enough to escort me to the front entrance, where I waited for Jason.

In a few minutes, my phone rang. It was Jason, calling to tell me that something suddenly came up and he would miss our match. Of course! I knew this was code for, "I don't want to get beat today, so I'm calling to make up a lame excuse." That put a damper on my afternoon exercise. As I thought about what to do instead, I saw a manager coming towards me. "Hi, my name is Scotty and I was wondering if you could help me with a recommendation."

"My pleasure," Jonathan said. "What might that be?"

"I had a tennis match scheduled for this afternoon, but my buddy didn't want me to beat the pants off him and he canceled. Could you suggest another activity for me?"

"Scotty, if you have your heart set on a tennis match, I get off work in 15 minutes. I would be happy to give you a go." Perfect, a match was on.

I hustled back towards my room, through the lobby and into the elevator, where I pushed the button and was whisked away to the 10th floor. When the shiny doors opened, I stepped out, making a quick right and an immediate left. Who do you think I saw in the hallway again? No, it was not Claudia. The hallway was empty. However, because of the spectacular service I had been receiving, I half-expected Serena Williams or Rafael Nadal to be there with some pointers for my match. Not so much.

Jonathan and I began our match and let me tell you, this young man was good, really good. I do not think I won more than two points per game. I wondered why, as a Ritz employee, he was not letting me win just so I would feel good. Then it hit me. Perhaps Jonathan read my profile in the Ritz CRM and figured out that I am a competitive person. He would know that I play golf, wrote a book, and was training for an Ironman. He also probably remembered my comment about wanting to beat the pants off Jason. Jonathan knew, instead of letting me win, the only thing that would get my competitive juices going was a knock-down, drag-out match. For all my smack throughout the day, in the end, it was Jonathan who beat the pants off me.

Back to the room for a shower and a power nap. Since I had such an enjoyable meal the previous night, I dined again at the Grill Room. Walking around the complex after dinner, I enjoyed the perfect weather, 72 degrees and not even a hint of humidity. The evening was awesome, with stars dotting the black sky like diamonds.

During my walk, I stopped at one of the outside lounges where I met Mike. We talked for a little while and I learned that Mike had worked at the Ritz for nearly a decade. "I'm doing some research about spectacular customer service," I told him. "Would you happen to have any stories you can share with me?"

"Absolutely," Mike replied, "Thomas the Train."

A young couple, let's call them Grace and John, came to the Ritz Carlton for vacation, bringing their son, Kevin, with them. As with most two-year-olds, Kevin had a favorite toy. His was Thomas the Train, who went everywhere with him. While staying at the Ritz, the family, along with Thomas the Train, went to the amusement parks, the water parks, and everywhere in between. On the day they were to fly home, Grace and John noticed that Thomas the Train was missing. Panic ensued. They knew what Kevin's reaction would be, so an all-points bulletin went out. Ritz employees helped scour the property, but with no luck. Kevin left without Thomas the Train.

The team at the Ritz Carlton decided to do something about this unfortunate incident. Wanting to create a lasting memory for the family, several employees went to a local toy store where they purchased a brand-new Thomas the Train, along with a scrapbook. They took Thomas the Train to the Ritz pool, the spa, and the golf course, snapping photos the entire way. Putting the pictures in the scrapbook with clever captions, they shipped it all to Kevin via overnight delivery, along with this letter. "Dear Kevin, your Thomas the Train decided to stay with us for a few extra days. We thought you might like these photographs to keep as memories. Hope to see you again soon."

When that family opened the package and saw Thomas the Train, the scrapbook and the letter, I imagine that their reaction was the same as the service they encountered during their stay. Spectacular!

I said goodbye to Mike and retired to my room for the evening. I thought about the incredible service that I had received from all the Ritz employees. In every instance, they anticipated my needs and exceeded my expectations. When all was said and done, they transformed me into a customer for life.

INSURANCE (SWING AND A MISS)

Not everything is rainbows and unicorns. Unfortunately, the likelihood of receiving spectacular service is not as prevalent as we would like it to be. Average service seems to be the standard, but there are still too many poor customer service experiences in the world. The good news is that we can still learn from those experiences and improve on them. Here is one encounter that could use some tweaks.

After selling a vehicle recently, I called my insurance agency to cancel the policy. "You're due a refund," the agent said. "You've already paid for a full year. We'll process the paperwork and you'll have a refund check within two weeks."

That was easy, but I was surprised that the agent did not ask about a future vehicle. Would I need to insure another car, and could he help me with that? I had been with the company for almost a decade. Were they not interested in keeping my business? Oh, well. I guess they had so much business that I was just another daily transaction.

Three weeks went by and I did not have a check, nor any word from my insurance company. I had not followed up on it because I was not counting on the refund to pay bills, but if you tell a customer that you are going to do something in two weeks, then you should do it. Or at least make a phone call and let the client know you need more time. The last thing you want is the customer contacting you about a blown deadline.

When I called to ask where my check might be, I learned that it was sent to my old address, the one I had three years ago. Ok, I get it. Mistakes happen. The agent updated my address and said another check would be sent out either that day or the next, and I would have it within two weeks. No problem, but one suggestion would be to add a procedure to confirm a client's address before sending a refund check. That would probably save a lot of phone calls and a bunch of disappointed customers.

Another two weeks went by and again, no check. I called the insurance company to let them know that I had still not received the refund. I wondered what would have happened if the situation had been reversed? Suppose I mailed a premium payment, but put the wrong address on the envelope and it never arrived? I guarantee that I would have been assessed late fees or even had my policy canceled.

At this point, five weeks had gone by since I first contacted the insurance agency, so I called the owner. He sincerely apologized. I asked him why it was up to me to track down my refund. "Not one of your agents has called me to see if I received the check," I said, "and I haven't heard a peep from you, either." He told me that because they have so many checks going out, it is impossible to proactively call clients to see if they received their refund. There is only time to deal with the customers who phone to complain.

This seemed like a missed opportunity to call up a client and engage in a conversation with the goal of transforming a transaction into a relationship. When things are going well, these are only transactions, but when things go badly, you don't have a solution except to wait for the customer to call you? I doubt this was the first incident of a missing refund check. How about implementing one of these solutions? Perhaps, after the first lost check, make it standard operating procedure to send the replacement via overnight delivery. Or, even better, if you have more checks going out than you can keep up with, analyze why that is. Evaluate why customers request refunds and put procedures in place to mitigate the pain points for the client and the company.

In today's world, people are looking for great service, a memorable experience, and convenience. Seamless, efficient business processes go a long way in satisfying those demands. Review your procedures on a regular basis to keep your customers from switching to your competitors. That is exactly what happened in my case. I took my insurance business to a competitor because of poor customer service.

CARMAX (THAT WAS EASY)

Sooner or later, most of us have to purchase a car, which is something I hate to do. You go to a dealer's lot and a salesperson immediately rushes up to you as if you are a long-lost cousin. When you find a vehicle you like, the next step is negotiating the price, a process that gives me nightmares. The associate goes back and forth between you and a manager who seems to be hidden in a back room somewhere. After five or six trips to the mystery manager, the salesperson finally says, "This is our lowest price and we're losing money on the deal." The experience I had with CarMax was just the opposite. Here is what happened.

Before going car shopping, I wanted to do some research online, so one Saturday afternoon I looked at the CarMax website. They have about a million vehicles. Surely there is one that is right for me, but can I find it from my couch while watching a golf tournament on TV?

I downloaded the CarMax app to my phone and saw the filter button right away. By choosing the features that I wanted on a car, I could narrow the field. I made my selections and seven vehicles popped up. Two were in my area, but the rest were some distance away. Would I have to travel to see the car I wanted? Nope!

CarMax lets you request a transfer of certain vehicles to a closer location for no charge. Wait just a minute. How much is this going to cost me? Do I have to enter my credit card to have this initiated? Do I have to commit to purchasing the car? These were just some of the "got ya" questions that were going through my mind, so I dug a little deeper. For cars within a certain distance, there is no charge for a transfer. Beyond that distance, there is a cost and you see the amount before you request the transfer. And... there is no obligation to purchase the car. CarMax will hold the vehicle for up to seven days while you decide.

I liked what I had learned so far, and still had not left my couch, so I filled out the transfer form and hit submit. A minute or two later, my phone rang. It was CarMax. Thanking me for requesting a transfer, the associate explained how the process would work. The communication was incredible. I received an email notification when the car was put on a trailer, when it was shipped, and when it arrived in my city. This shopping experience was becoming fun. When the vehicle was ready, a sales associate phoned to schedule a test drive.

When I arrived on the lot, not a single salesperson tried to break the 100-meter-dash record by running up to me. I checked in, an associate made a copy of my driver's license, and we hit the road. After the test drive, we sat down in the office and talked about next steps. Because the vehicle was exactly what I wanted, I was ready to make a deal, but without the negotiating process that gives me nightmares. The associate showed me to a computer where I answered a few simple questions on the screen, such as whether I wanted an extended warranty, would I be trading in a vehicle, and would I need CarMax to get the tags.

The final steps were all mine, which were to make sure I had insurance on the car and bring in a check. The sales associate mentioned that CarMax could provide financing if I needed it. Excellent upsell opportunity. I arranged for insurance on the vehicle and took a check to CarMax the next day. Done!

During this entire process, I noticed that CarMax linked some emotions to the buying experience. They made me happy (especially because I could do the initial shopping from my couch) and I felt relief that the sales negotiation was so easy and straightforward. When you link an emotion to an experience, you can help transform a transaction into a relationship. Thank you, CarMax, for providing me with that incredible experience.

APPLE (ARE THEY PSYCHIC?)

I needed a new iPhone. Mine was an early model that had served me well, but when it took three hours to download the movie Top Gun, it was time for an upgrade.

The online ordering process on the Apple website was easy and took maybe two minutes. Incredible. At the end of the process, this question popped up on the screen, "Would you like to trade in your old phone for a credit?" Of course I would. Who needs two phones?

After clicking yes, I was asked for the serial number of my trade-in phone. Ha! No way, no how, I knew where this secret number was hidden. I hesitated. Would the credit be worth what was sure to be a frustrating search? I almost gave up right there, but then this message came up, "If you don't know your serial number, or don't know where to find it, click here." Excellent anticipation. I followed the instructions, entered the serial number to get the trade-in credit, and received a confirmation that my iPhone would be delivered in two weeks.

Three days later, my new phone arrived, more than a week early. Apple had underpromised and overdelivered. Just four clicks and 30 minutes of downloading later, my data was transferred from the old phone to the new one.

My new screen said, "Are you ready?" Absolutely, so I pushed the button marked yes. Right at that moment, my doorbell rang. It was my UPS dude, Nick, standing at the door with a box. Not just any box, but the one I was to use to send my trade-in phone to

Apple. Is the service that good? Is Apple psychic, or was this only a coincidence? I will leave that up to you to decide.

Either way, this experience was fantastic and felt as if it was customized specifically for me. The service was spectacular, the experience was excellent, and the convenience was lightning fast. By having these components in your business, you will be able to stand out from your competition instead of blending in.

DOCTORS AND NURSES

I was on mile 122.6 with only 18 to go to complete my first Ironman event. Feeling my heart rate creep up, I slowed down to a walk and took my pulse. 188…not good. Five minutes later, I took it again. 180…better, but still not good. Continuing to walk, I started to feel better at mile 128.6, which was where I met my friends.

The first was Kristina. She wanted to run with me, but I told her I needed to keep walking, so we just talked for a bit about what it would feel like when I finished the race. Next were Andy, Bronco, Katie and Sheena. They gave me a bunch of high-fives and made me feel great. My friends back home, Jess, Cameron and Alicia, were giving me encouragement online. Then there was Chris. He wanted to make sure I had a plan to finish. He did all the mathematical calculations and gave me a specific strategy to finish the last 12 miles. It worked perfectly, and I completed my first Ironman.

Before we go on, I would like to thank all my friends who supported me throughout my training and at the event. I seriously believe it is just as hard to be a spectator for an Ironman event as it is to participate and complete one. Thank you all from the bottom of my new heart.

Completely exhausted from the race, I took a few weeks off from my exercise routine, then ventured back to the treadmill. Two minutes in, I felt a pain shoot from my right ear, through my chin, and to my left ear. Strange. I have a high pain tolerance, but this downright hurt. Backing off my pace, I walked for a few minutes, then took the treadmill up to a blistering six miles per hour. I know, I know. Two minutes later, the pain came back. Was my body telling me that I was still in Ironman recovery mode and should take another week off? I went with that theory.

Fast forward to the next week. I was in San Diego, waiting for an elevator to take me to my hotel room. Wait a minute, my room is on the second floor and I am waiting for an elevator? I am an Ironman, take the steps, you big baby. I turned around and started bounding up the steps two at a time. When I got to the second floor, that pain came back. Uh-oh.

When I got back to Orlando, I thought I would give it one more try and hopped on the treadmill. At exactly two minutes, the pain came back, feeling like a knot in my chest. Time to get help.

My next stop was a visit to a cardiologist. When Dr. Layeni ordered an immediate heart catheterization, I was certain of two things. This physician offered spectacular service, and I had a serious problem.

Before the heart cath started, I was warned that depending on what the doctor found, I may need a stent, a tiny tube that props open arteries. I know plenty of people my age who have had stents implanted, so that possibility did not seem too scary. After someone injected me with a blue dye, we were underway. I drifted in and out of sleep during the procedure, but still knew what was going on the entire time. It was not long before I heard Dr. Layeni say, "We have good news and bad news. Which would you like first?" At that point, I was after all the good news I could get. "Okay," he said, "the good news is that you don't need any stents." Great! Then I remembered that bad news was coming. "All of your arteries are clogged. You'll need emergency open heart surgery as soon as possible." Damn.

"Scott, good afternoon, my name is Dr. Allen. I will be your heart surgeon." The operation was scheduled for the very next morning. These people were not kidding around. Dr. Allen explained what would happen during the surgery. Until then, I thought a quintuple by-pass was the most you could do. I guess I win the prize for what my friend, Leo, calls "The Full Monty." I needed six by-passes.

As I laid awake in the hospital bed that night, a sense of calm came over me. I was in good hands. and there was nothing I could do about the situation anyway. When I phoned my family and friends to tell them the news, they were more shocked than I was. After all, I finished an Ironman, exercised six days a week, and ate reasonably well (maybe this last one is up for debate).

I was rolled into the operating room bright and early. The anesthesiologist filled me in on what was next, and the nurses said they would see me in about five hours. I looked at the clock on the wall. It was 7 a.m., so I set my sights on noon. I was told there would be a breathing tube down my throat when I woke up. "Don't pull it out," the nurse warned. "Most patients try to, but leave it alone. I'll be right there to remind you to relax." I felt pretty helpless lying on that hard table, so I was grateful for her instructions. Looking back, I realize that everyone was carefully setting expectations for my experience, and it definitely helped.

The anesthesiologist was up next. "I need you to do something for me," he said.

If you haven't guessed by now, I am a competitive person. Although I like to win at everything, the competition is the fun part. This guy asked me to count backwards from 100. "What's the lowest number anyone has ever gotten to?" I asked him.

"88."

Hmmm...the number of keys on a piano. Game on. "I think I can get to 79," I said, a little too confidently as it turned out. A few days after the surgery, the anesthesiologist confirmed that I went under at 97. I lost, big time.

As soon as I went under, I woke right up...5 hours later. I could see a clock, 12:20 p.m. Right on time! Two nurses were standing over me, telling me to relax, which is not the easiest thing to do with a tube down your throat. They gave me a ten-question quiz requiring yes or no answers. I tried to use hand signals to reply, but it did not really matter. The nurses were smiling at me, the most powerful gesture in the world, so I drifted back to sleep.

I woke back up at 4 p.m. to the sight of two nurses who had smiles on their faces as if they just won the Powerball. We went through the same routine as before, but this time they were also giving me instructions as they removed the breathing tube.

The breathing tube came out with no problems and I had a bazillion questions. My first question was, "Why did this take so long? You mentioned that I would be awake by about noon, but after I woke up, you all kept the breathing tube in for another four hours." They assured me that this sometimes happens. When I first woke up, my blood pressure was not where they wanted it to be, so they needed to wait a few minutes before checking it again and taking the tube out. But then I fell back to sleep before they could give it another try. Not wanting to disturb me, the nurses decided to just monitor my blood pressure until I woke up again on my own. Even while I was sleeping, they were already thinking about how to improve my experience. Pretty cool.

They wheeled me into the Intensive Care Unit, where I would stay until I was stable enough to go a regular patient room. One by one, the entire surgery team came in to tell me that everything went perfectly. It cannot get any better than that! Maybe it was the pain medication, or the phenomenal personal attention I was getting, or the fact that I had a second chance at life, but I felt like the most important person in the world.

I met a new team member who would take control of the situation from then until I left the hospital. Her name was Janel, a key individual who helped me get back to my old self. In short order, Janel figured out my entire life story. She knew I was competitive, enjoyed making people laugh, and wanted to return to my active life style as soon as possible. She said that the first step was to get to the point where she could remove the three chest tubes that were sticking out of me. Those things looked like garden hoses. Janel gave me a list of things that I needed to accomplish over the next three days and if did all of them, she would remove the chest tubes. Yay!

Finally, everything on the list was complete. Janel said it was go time, but it would hurt and hurt bad. The last time I heard someone say that, I was in a fight with the kid who sat behind me in fourth grade. Now it was coming from a nurse. Not a good sign. Janel wrapped her hand around the tubes as close to my chest as possible. She wanted to pull them entirely out in one motion. If she had to regrip and pull a second time, who knows how loud the screams would be. "I'll count to three," she said, "then I'll pull. You'll probably pass out."

No way, not me. I am not passing out just because someone is pulling three plastic tubes out of my chest. Bring it on, Janel.

"Ready?" she asked. "One…." And then she yanked all three tubes out at once. She tricked me. I woke up about 30 minutes later, wondering what in the hell just happened.

The entire process in the ICU seemed focused on me. The attention to detail was unbelievable and the nurses made me feel as if I were one of the team. By kindly encouraging me to talk about things I enjoy, the staff helped me stay upbeat and be confident about recovery. Improving my hospital experience helped improve my health. That is the epitome of spectacular customer service.

The staff on the regular floors were just as focused on patient care as the team in the ICU. Their goal was to make sure that I was healthy enough to go home soon. This meant I had to start eating and walking around the floor, but not at the same time.

Janel carved out a plan for me. It would take effort and the support of the team around me, but if we could make it happen, I would go home in three days. The first order of business was to start eating. I had already lost 15 pounds (I would not recommend having six arterial bypasses to lose weight). My first meal was delivered and I lifted the lid on the tray. "What in the world are these?" I asked the nutritionist.

"They are good for you. Just eat them."

I tried one more time, saying, "I'm not comfortable eating anything I've never seen before. I'm sure they're good for me, but what are they called?"

Giving me a wry smile, the nutritionist said, "Vegetables!"

I listened to the experts and started eating these newly discovered food items. Soon, I had the energy to start the next phase of recovery, exercise, which did not mean hitting the leg press machine or anything like that. This exercise was walking. Piece of cake, I thought. Our goal was to walk at least three times a day, as far as I could without getting totally exhausted. The first time I made it a whole 27 feet.

The staff encouraged me every day, and the doctor gave the okay for me to go home according to plan. It felt like an incredible achievement, however, I knew there were more obstacles to overcome and I would not be able to do it alone. As much as this is a story of spectacular service from every single person at the hospital, it is also a reminder that life is precious, and we should cherish the people around us. It sure is nice to have them in our lives.

FREEDOM BOAT CLUB (I GOT YA!)

I made the deal of the century! Last year I purchased 117 boats here in Florida for $275.44 per month. I know it sounds too good to be true, but strap in because you are going to love this story.

My friend Terry and his wife Lisa invited me to go boating. We drove to a dock in Jacksonville where their boat was all shined up and ready to go. After loading the stuff we needed for a day on the water, we took off with Terry at the helm. It was a perfect day. Cruising down the St. John's River, we stopped at a waterfront restaurant for lunch and had a delicious meal. Sun-soaked and relaxed when we got back to the dock, we grabbed our gear, tipped a couple of dock hands, and headed home.

Since I enjoy being on the water, I had been thinking about buying a boat, but did not want everything that comes with it. Like Terry, I just wanted the fun, not the maintenance and worry of ownership. Hello, Freedom Boat Club! As we drove home from our day on the river, Terry explained the membership benefits that the club offers. You can reserve a boat in any of the locations across the country. There is no storage fee, no maintenance fee, no cleaning the boat before or after you put it in the water. If the boat needs repairs, you do not pay for that either. Even if a breakdown happens on the water, a service is dispatched to help you at no charge. All this seemed too good to be true.

The next weekend I drove to my local Freedom Boat Club to check things out. The first person I met there was Thomas. He was friendly, professional and an absolute expert at his job. After taking down my information, Thomas set me up with a complimentary ride with another gentleman, Tom. While we took a short boat tour, Tom explained the membership options, which were easy to understand. There was a small initiation fee, then a monthly cost of $275. I was sold.

My maiden voyage as a Freedom Boat Club member was the following weekend. Setting me up with everything I needed for an afternoon on the water, Thomas said to call him when I was ready to come in and he would take care of the rest. Off I went, navigating a series of lakes until I reached my own neighborhood, where I showed the boat to a couple of friends. They were excited to plan an excursion. Returning to the dock, I mentioned to Thomas that I was going to make an online reservation to take my buddies out the next weekend. He volunteered to take care of that for me and we said our goodbyes.

When my friends and I arrived at the dock the next Saturday, Thomas greeted all of us by name. Wow! That was impressive and put smiles on our faces. After the boat ride, Thomas asked us how it went and if he could do anything in the future to improve our experience. "Yes," I said, "Clone yourself." Thomas offered to make another reservation for us, but I declined because I had some traveling coming up. "I'll set something up when I get back," I told him.

A lot happened in the next few weeks. An uninvited guest named Irma barreled through Florida as a Category 4 hurricane, ripping off roofs, flooding cities and obliterating small towns. Anything that dared get in her way was wiped out, including our local Freedom Boat Club.

Fast forward a few weeks and who is calling me? Thomas. He wanted to let me know that the boat dock had been destroyed in the hurricane, but the club was exploring options to relocate a few miles away. He would keep me up to date on when they were back in business. Talk about someone being proactive. That does not happen very often. Usually it is the customer calling to ask what is going on. Thomas anticipated a customer need and acted accordingly.

A few weeks later, Thomas phone again. Whoop, whoop! Time to go boating again! I met Thomas and Tim at the new facility. These guys were awesome. Every time I needed something, Tim would help. If Tim was busy working with another client, Thomas would say "I got ya."

I know what you are thinking. What about the 117 boats I purchased? That is actually the number of vessels that are available with my membership level. I can reserve a boat when I am traveling, or I can use one from the many local clubs in Florida. Another great feature is that you can freeze your membership for a small fee, putting it on hold for a designated period.

For me, and many others, we join the Freedom Boat Club because the features and benefits are tremendous. We stay because of individuals like Thomas, who create client loyalty and retention by transforming everyday transactions into relationships.

HOME DEPOT (LET ME GET THAT)

I decided to build a small beach at the end of my property. I had absolutely no idea what I was doing so I went to the place that has everything, YouTube. After watching a few videos, I felt like an expert so I started the process. The first step was getting the materials for a foundation, which meant a trip to Home Depot for a bunch of cinder blocks. By my mathematical calculations, I needed 24 blocks, but my SUV could only hold 12 at a time. I would have to make two trips. No problem.

When I arrived at the store, a clerk with a warm smile and a friendly hello greeted me. I asked where the concrete cinder blocks were located. "Aisle two," the lady said. Quite different than some other companies where they escort you to the items. Twelve blocks and what seemed like 10,000 calories later, I had everything stacked on one of Home Depot's bright orange carts. If I were the manager of that store, I would strategically place Advil right next to the heavy items to upsell to people like me. I headed to the check-out aisle and whizzed through in record time. When I got to my SUV to unload the blocks (why did it seem as if they were getting heavier?), that was when the service went from good, to great, to spectacular.

From out of nowhere, a clerk named Brendan appeared right next to my vehicle saying, "Excuse me, sir, can I give you a hand loading those blocks?" Who was I to say no? With Brendan outpacing me two blocks to one, we had them loaded in no time. What was impressive about Brendan's assistance was that he was working on another project in the parking lot when he noticed me pushing the cart to my vehicle. He anticipated my needs and reprioritized his responsibilities so he could help me load those heavy suckers. By going above and beyond and exceeding a client's expectations, Brendan transformed a good customer experience into a great one. I will make sure to look for him on my next trip to Home Depot.

SOUTHWEST AIRLINES (KICK TAIL®)

Kick Tail® is one of the most amazing employee loyalty programs that no one knows about.

I was on a Southwest flight, traveling from Alabama back home to Orlando. It was a milestone in my travels with the airline because it catapulted me to the next frequent flyer level, one that qualified me for the "companion pass." This pass lets another person accompany you for FREE on all your trips for an entire year. You can change your companion throughout the year, spreading the love to different people. Because I wanted to document this achievement, the captain invited me into the cockpit for a photograph. The image had the most views of anything I posted on Twitter that year. Thanks, Southwest Airlines.

My friend Rick is also a Southwest frequent flyer, with way more miles than I have. While visiting him in Texas, Rick offered me a few drink tickets to use on the flight home. I declined because I already had plenty of tickets, but then he said, "Take one of these." He handed me a Kick Tail®.

A Kick Tail® is like the Golden Ticket on Willy Wonka and the Chocolate Factory. It is a reward that customers can give to Southwest employees who deliver spectacular service. Kick Tail® recipients are entered into a drawing each month for a chance to win a host of prizes. The more Kick Tail® employees receive, the more chances they have. "This is perfect," I thought, "because now you have the passengers looking to give these away to employees who go above and beyond the call of duty." Excellent idea. Usually four Kick Tail® are given to passengers once they hit certain frequent flyer tiers with Southwest. I could not wait to get my own.

Later that month, I received four Kick Tail® and thought intently about how I would give them out. Every employee at Southwest seems to exceed expectations, so my decision was harder than I thought it would be. Then it hit me while I was waiting for my luggage at the Orlando baggage claim. In all my travels on Southwest, my bags have never been lost or delayed. This trip was no exception. After collecting my bags from the conveyor belt, I went into the baggage claim office where I was greeted with a pleasant smile. I told the Southwest employee that I received my bags right on time, just like always, and wanted to say thank you. "I can only imagine the feeling that passengers have when their bags are delayed or misplaced," I said, "and I'm certain that you do everything in your power to help them. I would like to give you this Kick Tail® for two reasons. First, for helping all those people every day, and second, here's hoping, in a nice way, that I never have to visit this office looking for my bags."

MARRIOTT (SKILLET MEATBALLS)

I was traveling to Orange County, California, to open a new franchise location. I always look forward to these visits because I get to meet new franchise owners and, in a small way, help them grow their business. I booked my flight through Southwest Airlines and reserved a room at the Marriott.

Since my flight was a little early, I decided to check into the hotel first. Marriott's exceptional customer service started as soon as I walked through the automatic doors, with employees greeting me with warm smiles and friendly hellos. While checking me in, the receptionist thanked me for being a Platinum member and offered a complimentary beverage. I got settled in, then went to meet the new franchise owner.

After a couple of hours and a productive strategy session with my client, I headed back to the Marriott. As soon as I arrived, as if on cue, my stomach started to growl. It was time for dinner. Although it was only mid-afternoon, California time is three hours earlier than I am used to. Rather than go out for a meal, I decided to try the hotel's new Bistro restaurant.

"What would you like this evening?" the gentleman asked as I approached the counter. When I requested a recommendation, he suggested the Skillet Meatballs straightaway, almost as if he received a commission for that item. "They are out of this world," he told me.

I took his suggestion, adding a Caesar Salad and a sweet iced tea, then patiently awaited my dinner. A few minutes later, the

Skillet Meatballs arrived, still sizzling hot. Letting those little nuggets of meat cool, I dusted off the Caesar Salad while watching a football game on TV. The time of reckoning came soon. I munched on the first meatball and was immediately disappointed. Disappointed because they were so scrumptious, but there were only five on the plate. I wanted 100 of those suckers! I thanked the chef and headed back to my room for the evening.

The next morning, I woke up early because my body was still not used to the time change. After a workout, shower, and breakfast, I met my client so we could go on some sales calls together. We spent the entire day introducing our business to potential customers. I enjoy this type of work because face-to-face interactions build more personal relationships than emails and texts do.

Arriving back at the hotel, I wondered what I should have for dinner. There was no thinking about it. The obvious answer was…Skillet Meatballs. I grabbed the room telephone and pressed what I thought was the button for the Bistro. Someone answered saying, "Mr. Werner, if you will hold on for one minute, we will be right with you." Cool, they used my name, which made me feel great. Just then, I looked down at the phone and realized that I had dialed the front desk by mistake. I hung up, pushed the button for the Bistro, and placed my order for those tasty Skillet Meatballs. As soon as I hung up, the phone rang. Hmmm, who could this be? It was the front desk manager. Uh-oh, what did I do wrong?

"I saw that you were put on hold, Mr. Werner, then we lost the call. What can we do for you? Is there still something you need?"

Wait just a minute! The manager is proactively calling me back to make sure that I had everything I needed? How often does such a thing happen? No need to reply, I know the answer to that question. Never.

After flying back across the country and landing in Orlando, I received an email from the general manager of the Marriott, thanking me for my stay. The customer experience was spectacular, making me feel as if I were the most important person on the property.

SPLASHEO (IT'S DONE?)

I waited as long as I could before moving into the 21st century when it comes to video technology. My VHS/BETA and 8mm equipment were not going to work for video on any of today's social media platforms.

When I need a recommendation, I usually go to one of my friends. This case was no exception. "Who do I know who speaks well, has lots of followers on social media, and creates powerful and professional videos?" I wondered. Easy, my friend Tim.

Tim put me in touch with Gideon Shalwick, the founder of Splasheo, a video captioning and editing service. I explained to Gideon that I wanted to serve up customized, attention-grabbing videos that support my business and attract viewers. I also shared what I did not want to do, which was spend tedious hours trying to learn editing software only to get mediocre results. "You've come to the right place," Gideon replied.

I pulled up the Splasheo website and saw the seven-day free trial. Free sounded like a good price to start so I created an account and logged on. A live-chat box popped up right away, with Amy asking what she could help me with. Wow, this was a great experience so far. I responded that I was just getting set up. Amy let me know that if I needed anything, she was only a few clicks away. After watching the cool tutorial, I was ready to give Splasheo a try with one of my YouTube videos.

The first step was to choose a template, which was easy and required almost zero effort on my part. Each one comes with a short instructional video that tells you what platform the template is designed for. Because I planned to share the videos primarily on LinkedIn, I chose a template customized for that social media outlet. Next, Splasheo walked me through selecting a format, along with primary and accent colors for my brand. Piece of cake, and so far, stress free. There were a few more customization tabs I could have used, but that was all I needed for this first video.

The only thing left to do was hit the submit button. I hovered my mouse above the button, took a deep breath, and clicked. You know how you always get those red messages when you fill out an online form? The ones that say you forgot the zip code, or you forgot to put in the CCV number, or you did not include what year you graduated kindergarten? I was prepared for a couple of red fields, but I received zero, zip. I was all done! If this company wanted to create an experience that was stress free and required almost no effort on my part, they sure accomplished their goal.

As soon as I clicked submit, I received a friendly email thanking me for my order and stating that technicians were already working on it. This made me feel important, as if I were building a relationship with the Splasheo team. The email included a sentence that made me smile, "We will have your video completed and back to you within 24 hours." I was skeptical of that part.

The next morning, I woke up early, did a little stretching, went for a run, then had breakfast. I try to make sure that I have crossed off a couple tasks on my to-do list before checking email or social media. When I fired up my laptop, there was a message from Splasheo at the top of my inbox. Ok, what did I do wrong? Did I pick the wrong colors? Did my video fail to upload? Was I not annunciating my words correctly? What was this problem going to be that I had to solve? I opened the email. "Hi Scotty, here is the link to download your captioned video." Incredible!

The finished product was perfect. The colors were crisp, the words flowed across the screen at the right cadence, and the video looked professional. Splasheo, you now have a new client.

If I had to sum up my experience in three words, it would be this: underpromise and overdeliver. At each stage in the process, my expectations were exceeded. By listening to what is important to their clients, Splasheo has created a user experience that feels customized and stress free.

TIME SAVER (CALL ME)

Currently, I think you must have three things to stay ahead of your competition. You need to offer spectacular service, create a great customer experience, and make it convenient and easy for clients to do business with you. Sometimes, it is not only management and employees that contribute to these advantages, but also the tools that companies give their teams to use. Let me explain.

I needed to make some adjustments to travel plans that I had booked in advance. Hotel reservations, plane tickets and rental cars all needed to be changed. First, I went to Marriott's website. A couple of clicks here, a couple of clicks there, and I was done. It was easy and a great customer experience. Next, I had to call Southwest Airlines because I had purchased a bargain ticket that could only be changed by talking with customer service. Perfectly understandable. Because SWA representatives are always courteous, professional and fun, I do not mind calling them. I have SWA on speed dial, so I hit the number and my smart phone dialed away.

Instead of an agent, I got a voice message saying that I was calling during a busy time and my hold would be about six minutes. I was welcome to wait, or I could type in my phone number and get a call back when an agent was available. I would not even lose my place in the queue. I know from experience that just like dog years, six minutes on hold can feel like four hours. Why in the world would I not choose the call-back option? I typed in my phone number to get a return call. This was great because instead of waiting on hold, I could work on a chapter of this book, or I could shoot another video. No matter what I did, it would be more productive than waiting on hold. To SWA's credit, my phone did ring in in about six minutes and the agent took of care of everything I needed. A fantastic experience.

The final change was for my car rental. Just like the plane ticket, I had gotten a special promotional price that could not be changed online. I would have to call customer service. No problem, I thought. They must have the same cool call-back feature that SWA has. Wrong!

As soon as I connected with the rental car company, a voice message let me know that I was calling during a busy time. Maybe someday I will learn when these busy times are. "Your wait time will be approximately 16 minutes," the voice said. We all know that 16 minutes can seem like eight days. Feeling lucky, I thought I would wait for a few minutes to see if an agent picked up. At the very least, I was sure that I would hear instructions for getting a call-back instead of waiting on hold. After four minutes, I gave up, with no agent and no opportunity to request a call back. Why not?

Does the car rental agency not know about technology that enables return calls? Maybe they know about it, but think it is too expensive. Whatever the reason, having to wait on hold made for a poor customer experience for me. When clients have a bad experience, 33% of the time they stop doing business with that company. That is exactly what I did.

PUBLIX (SHE FOUND ME)

I have always liked Publix grocery store. Friendly employees help you find things in the aisles and seem to genuinely care about helping you. The company often comes up with innovative ways to help customers save time and money, which are two things we could all use more of these days.

On a recent visit, I noticed some pre-made dinners in the meat section. Now in case you don't know, I am one of the pickiest people on the planet when it comes to trying a new food. It is not going to happen. However, if I see something I like and have had it before, and it only has a little twist, I will give it a try. On this day, my eyes locked on a pre-made dinner with scallops, shrimp and vegetables in a sweet chili sauce. It was only 10 bucks. I took this tasty dinner home, heated it up, added some Old Bay seasoning, then finished it off as if it were my last meal. It was phenomenal!

The next day, I woke up early, excited to go to Publix and stock up on these scrumptious dinners. I hopped in the car and drove the five miles to the store. In my excitement, I forgot to check the time. I guess I should have figured that Publix does not open at 5:45 a.m. I headed back home for a run, then to Publix again to pick up more of those dinners, lots of them.

This time around, I read the label on the package, learning that the meal had to be eaten within 24 hours and could not be frozen. That meant I could only buy one at a time, not the supply I had imagined. Darn. A thought did cross my mind. What if I purchased two, and had one for lunch and one for dinner? Too much of a good thing? Probably, so I only bought one.

About a week later, I got a hankering (my friend, Scotty J, from North Carolina, uses that term when his stomach is hungry for something specific) for another shrimp and scallop dinner in sweet chili sauce. Off to Publix again. An employee named Wendy was working the seafood counter and asked what she could make for me. When I told her what I wanted for dinner, she appeared sad, saying "Unfortunately, we're out of the sweet chili sauce. It won't be in until tomorrow." Now I was as sad as Wendy, but there are worse things in life, so I thanked her and said I would be back the next day. Twenty minutes later, however, I was still in the store, scouring the aisles for that evening's dinner. I felt a tap on my shoulder. Turning around, I saw Wendy.

While taking inventory in the freezer, Wendy noticed that a sauce was mislabeled and on the wrong shelf. It was none other than sweet chili sauce, the missing ingredient for my dinner. Wendy had searched for me in the aisles to let me know that she could take care of my order. Talk about making my day. She seemed to genuinely care about making my experience exceptional, and she certainly made that happen.

This goes to show you the difference between good service and spectacular service. Good service is taking care of what customers need. Spectacular service is going above and beyond and exceeding a customer's expectations. Wendy embodied this pinnacle of service.

FRESHLY (NO HUMANS?)

My friends are awesome. Since my heart surgery, they have been helping me find a way to eat these things that I have always avoided: vegetables. These vegetable things are supposed to be full of vitamins, minerals, and a host of other great things. After enough encouragement, I finally gave in. Scotty, meet Freshly.

My introduction to Freshly happened on a Memorial Day weekend, when I was helping my friend, Cameron, pour some concrete. Apparently, neither of us had anything better to do. We finished a small section at his house that required fourteen, 80-pound bags of concrete. The first seven bags didn't seem that heavy, but the last seven felt like 200 pounds each.

After we completed the project and admired our work, we grabbed some lunch, then headed back to the house. Cameron asked how it was going with my new-found nutritional goals. "Definitely a challenge on the vegetable front," I admitted. He said he had a solution for that problem in his refrigerator.

I went straight to his kitchen. The refrigerator was stocked with dinners with exciting descriptions like "Peppercorn Steak" and "Teriyaki Salmon Cakes," all from a company called Freshly. They sounded delicious. To thank me for the concrete work, Cameron cooked a fantastic ribeye steak for dinner that night.

As soon as I got home, I researched the company and confirmed everything Cameron told me about the service. I was ready to sign up. The first step was to download the Freshly app. Piece of cake.

Next, decide which meal-delivery program I wanted. If you are like me, you may be skeptical about agreeing to an ongoing service. Is there a contract? A cancellation fee? No such thing at Freshly. If I am going out of town, want to try to cook for myself, or for any other reason, all I need to do is click the skip button on the app. No meals are shipped and no fees are charged. Fantastic!

I chose the six-meal plan for $60 per week. Next came the fun part, selecting the actual dinners that I would receive. "This will be easy," I thought, "six Peppercorn Steaks." Done. But knowing the backlash I would get from my friends and heart surgeon, I expanded my selection to include some of those vegetable things.

So far, all of this was done on my phone through the Freshly app. No human contact. I learned from the app that I have until Wednesday of each week to make my meal choices, then the Freshly chefs go to work on my order. The meals arrive on my doorstep each Monday afternoon in a large box, packed with plenty of dry ice. I think they anticipate that the customers may not be home and want to make sure there is enough ice in case the package has to sit outside for a while.

I stored the meals in the refrigerator, heating them up for a couple of minutes in the microwave when I was ready for dinner. I ate all six. Not the same day! The next week, I varied my selections and the service repeated itself flawlessly.

From start to finish, Freshly made this a spectacular experience. The service was easy to use, the experience seemed customized, and the meals were incredible. They have earned my business. If anyone ever asks me what I am having for dinner, I will happily say, "A gourmet meal from Freshly!" Thank you, Freshly, and Cameron.

CARNIVAL CRUISE LINE

It was springtime and I was fortunate enough to be enjoying a cruise to the Bahamas with friends…for free. I went on a cruise earlier in the year and had a great time. This trip, however, was totally unexpected. Several people I work with purchased the cruise for me because I had helped them throughout the year. Although I was only doing my job, the gratitude that they showed me, and others, is nothing short of spectacular.

After boarding the ship, my friends and I enjoyed some frosty beverages while the luggage was loaded, then we were free to go to our rooms and get settled. We agreed to meet up later. When I got to my cabin, the door was slightly open, and I could see the steward inside, putting some finishing touches on my room. He was almost done making a towel animal, a clever trick that turns a common bath towel into a giraffe or some other creature. As the steward turned toward me, we stared at each other for a brief second. "Scotty!" he yelled.

I, in turn, screamed "Denny!"

I recognized Denny from my last cruise, but how did he remember me? After all, he had met hundreds of travelers since he last saw me. I do not think there is anything special about me, but there sure is something special about Denny.

We gave each other a high-five and started chatting. He asked if I was traveling with the same friends from last time. I told him no, this cruise I was with some people from work. Then Denny asked if I wanted him to make more towel animals for my cabin. That was a great question, and this is why he asked.

On my previous cruise, I was with friends who are as competitive as I am. We always find ourselves looking for bets to make with each other just to see who wins. When I first encountered Denny on that trip, he was in my cabin creating a towel animal, just like this time. "How many of those do you make for each cabin?" I asked him

"Just one per day," he replied, "but it is a different animal each time."

Ah ha! There was my first idea for a bet, complete with insider information as a prank on my buddies. I asked Denny if he could do me a favor and make all four animals on the first day. "Sure," he said, "but why?"

Letting him in on the plan, I explained that I was going to propose a wager to my friends: Who has the most towel animals made up in their cabin today? With Denny's help, I would have a distinct advantage for this bet. When my buddies and I compared photographs of our towel animals as proof, I would have four, thanks to Denny's handiwork, and everyone else would have only one. Denny got a kick out of it. "No problem," he said.

The fact that Denny remembered my wager from a few months ago was impressive. He took the time to ask questions about what was important to me, while actively listening so he would remember what I said. When you take time to put others first and are genuine and authentic, the result can be the start of a great relationship. Thank you, Denny, for delivering spectacular service to me, and, I am certain, to thousands of others just as fortunate.

AMEX (WE WILL FIND A SOLUTION)

I have used American Express credit card services for more than 30 years. It has been a phenomenal experience. Here is just one example of why AmEx has retained my business for over three decades.

I had taken advantage of a competitor's 0% financing offer which, after 18 months, was now coming due. I know you are thinking that nothing is free and there must be a transaction cost, and you would be correct. But paying only a 2% transaction fee for 18 months was a huge benefit for me at the time.

Knowing that the bill was coming due, I was prepared to pay it off, almost. Sometimes life gets in the way of any well-crafted plan and my situation was no exception. I needed another 30 to 45 days. It was not a big deal if I did not get the extra time, but I would have to pay interest on the balance until it was paid off. If that happened, the credit card company would win this round.

I thought about how I could avoid the additional fees, and then it hit me, AmEx. In the past, whenever I needed assistance, AmEx had a solution. I logged into my account to look for any new promotional offers. Bingo! There was a tab labeled balance transfer. I know, I know. You are thinking that I am going to be stuck in a perpetual balance transfer wormhole where I am paying 2% every 18 months and never paying down my balance. Ah, you could be right.

I clicked on the balance transfer button and reviewed the offers, but nothing fit my situation. Continuing the search until I exhausted my options, I called AmEx and reached Chris, the man who was going to fix everything.

What a nice person. We chatted for a few minutes, then Chris said, "Mr. Werner, how can I help you?" I told him about my search and learned that those balance transfer offers are sent out according to some specific criteria and apparently, I did not qualify. Then he asked me a great question. "Mr. Werner, do you mind if I ask you a few questions so I can understand exactly what you are trying to accomplish? I'm certain we can find a solution for you."

This was nothing short of incredible. For the first time in a decade, someone asked me if it was okay to continue the conversation. And, Chris gave me a reason why I should keep talking with him. I had time, so I said, "Sure, ask away."

By asking me a series of open-ended questions, Chris peeled back the curtain on what I really needed. Recommending a product that was an ideal match, he walked me through the sign-up process. Five minutes later, my problem was solved.

Chris took extra time to find out specifically what I was looking for and how he could help. This transformed the transaction into a relationship, cementing the reason that I have been an AmEx client for so long. Thank you, Chris, and the entire AmEx team for delivering spectacular service.

TOP CUSTOMER SERVICE TIPS

Sometimes big things come in small packages. You can make significant improvement to customer experience without any financial investment or major overhauls. Try these tips for how to implement some of the top customer service techniques in your company.

HOW TO REMEMBER NAMES

When I speak at conferences, many people come up to me and say, "Scotty, I know I am supposed to use a person's name in order to build a relationship, but I'm not good at remembering names."

I get it. I had difficulty remembering names until I figured out a best practice that helped me become better at it. Give this technique a try and see how it works for you.

When someone asks an open-ended question, we tend to answer too quickly. For example, if an acquaintance says, "How was your weekend?" my old habit would be to launch into a description of what I did. What I have learned to do, instead, is embrace a slight pause, use the person's name, then take my time to reply with a short sentence. I can go into detail later. The exchange may sound something like this:

"Scotty, how was your weekend?"

"Andy, it was awesome!" Then I can give Andy the details that made the weekend memorable.

Practice this technique and you will become better at remembering names and building relationships.

HOW TO STOP SAYING I'M SORRY

While out and about this weekend, I must have heard the words "I'm sorry" a dozen times. On one occasion, a server got my order wrong, saying "I'm sorry" while smiling and laughing. It sounded meaningless and inappropriate. We should use sorry for serious things, not every time there is a small mistake.

This best practice replaces the word sorry with empathy, follow up, and an apology. Imagine that you are a call center professional with an angry customer on the phone. The customer was charged a $29 late fee in spite of having a cancelled check proving that the payment was received on time. After you have actively listened to the customer, try this response.

"Mr. Parker, I understand your frustration and I'm sure this isn't a pleasant call for you to make. Thank you for bringing this to our attention. I will investigate immediately and call you back in one hour. Even if I don't have an answer, I'll give you an update about what I've learned. I appreciate you taking time out of your day to make us aware of this problem, as I'm sure there are more important things you could be doing. Also, I'll look at our procedures to see if we need to make some internal changes so this doesn't happen to anybody else. Mr. Parker, thank you for calling us. We appreciate your business and I'll call you back in one hour with an update. "

By showing empathy, following up, and apologizing, you will be able to transform an angry customer into a happy one without saying sorry.

HOW TO SAY THANK YOU

Do you still go to your mailbox every day? I do, but it is a mundane task. In the last 30 years, I have not found much that makes me smile when I pull out all the junk. Other than routine bills, my mail is mostly letters telling me that I have been "approved" for a two-billion-dollar loan, or coupons for the latest product on the market, which at the time of this writing was diet ice water.

I have developed a habit that makes my daily mailbox trip more satisfying: sending handwritten thank you notes to clients, employees and friends. It takes me about 30 minutes a week to write the cards, and what an awesome feeling when I drop them in the mailbox. My friend Tim says, "Gratitude is a muscle and you should exercise that muscle on a regular basis." This best practice for saying thank you has helped me feel great, cement relationships, and differentiate myself from the competition.

Every Monday, I put a blank piece of paper on a clipboard, titling it "Thank You Cards for the Week." Nothing fancy, just a sheet of notebook paper. I could create a document on my computer but keeping the list in front of me reminds me to use it. As the week goes along, I add names of the people I want to personally thank, ranging from clients to employees and friends. On Friday mornings, I write the notes around 8 a.m., before I get involved in other tasks. Now these are not ten-page novels, only a few sentences to say thank you, along with a personalized a message.

Try it out and you will have a new sense of appreciation when you go to your mailbox. And who knows? Maybe I will be fortunate enough to meet and work with you, and you will find one in your mailbox from me.

HOW TO ACTIVELY LISTEN

Like most people, I find myself wanting to talk instead of listening when I am in a conversation. While the other person is speaking, I pick up on cues and start formulating my response. Once I start thinking about what I am going to say, I hardly pay any attention to what the conversation is about. I finally realized how inconsiderate this habit is to other individuals.

With the help of my friends, I have learned to actively listen. Here is a best practice that helps me stay more engaged when I talk with friends and colleagues. Give it a try for yourself.

When your conversation partner is through speaking, say something like, "Tell me a little more about that," before launching into your response. You can use whatever question you like, but make sure it is not a closed-ended one. Yes and no answers tend to end an exchange quickly. Asking an open-ended question accomplishes a couple of things. First, it ensures that you continue to listen instead of talk. Second, you get to hear details that are important to the other person. In many cases, these details will help you pull back the curtain and discover the need that is behind the need.

Practice this concept to become a great listener and enjoy deeper, more meaningful conversations.

CUSTOMER SERVICE FACTS

Poor service is the number one reason customers give for leaving a company.

Customers feel a major reason for poor service is because they must repeat themselves.

33% of customers switch companies after only one bad experience.

64% of customers say that experience is more important than price when purchasing a product or service.

67% of customers mention bad experiences as a reason for leaving a company, however, only one in 26 who have a bad experience ever complain.

68% of clients say that a customer service representative was key to a positive experience.

72% of customers say that when contacting customer service, they expect the agent to know their name.

72% of businesses say improving customer service is their number one priority.

86% of customers are willing to pay more for a great experience.

90% of Americans use customer service as a factor in deciding whether to do business with a company.

90% of people want to talk and only 10% actively listen.

91% of customers stop using a product or service when they must repeat themselves to the customer service professional.

91% of customers who are unhappy with a brand will leave without complaining.

Companies that deploy a well-crafted customer service program enjoy a 92% customer retention rate.

It costs 700% more to acquire a new customer than it does to keep an existing one.

www.ingramcontent.com/pod-product-compliance
Lightning Source LLC
Chambersburg PA
CBHW030940240526
45463CB00015B/862